YOUR KNOWLEDGE HAS VALUE

Robotics and Autonomous Systems. Innovations, Challenges, and Future Prospects

Rajesh Kumar Mishra
Divyansh Mishra
Rekha Agarwal

Bibliographic information published by the German National Library:

The German National Library lists this publication in the National Bibliography; detailed bibliographic data are available on the Internet at http://dnb.dnb.de.

ISBN: 9783389117224
This book is also available as an ebook.

© GRIN Publishing GmbH
Trappentreustraße 1
80339 München

Print and binding: Books on Demand GmbH, Norderstedt, Germany
Printed on acid-free paper from responsible sources.

The present work has been carefully prepared. Nevertheless, authors and publishers do not incur liability for the correctness of information, notes, links and advice as well as any printing errors.

GRIN web shop: https://www.grin.com/document/1563344

Robotics and Autonomous Systems: Innovations, Challenges, and Future Prospects

[1]Department of Artificial Intelligence and Data Science
Jabalpur Engineering College
Jabalpur (MP)
[2]ICFRE-Tropical Forest Research Institute
(Ministry of Environment, Forests & Climate Change, Govt. of India)
P.O. RFRC, Mandla Road, Jabalpur, MP-482021, India
[3]Government Science College
Jabalpur, MP, India- 482 001

Introduction

The science of robotics deals with devices that carry out activities automatically or semi-automatically using preset, adaptive programming and algorithms. These devices, also referred to as robots, are either operated by humans or fully controlled by computer programs and algorithms. The construction, design, and programming of robots are all included in the broad idea of robotics. These robots interact directly with the actual world, and they are frequently used in place of people to carry out repetitive and boring jobs. Robots can be grouped according to their size, field of use, or objective. Robotics is only one aspect of automation. It indicates that a procedure is carried out entirely or in part without the need for human intervention. Instead, only electrical or mechanical devices and pre-programmed or adaptable computer programs are used to run the process. The term "predefined applications" refers to algorithms, where every operation is predetermined and carried out autonomously, irrespective of any unanticipated environmental changes. The ability of the algorithm to modify its behavior in response to modifications in the environment or process is known as adaptive automation. Since robots are typically a component of automated systems, robotics and automation go hand in hand. Even if automation can exist without robots and robots can be utilized with little to no automation in some situations, the two are like identical twins, each with their own unique personality.

Evolution of Robotics: From Early Machines to AI-Driven Systems

Automation, along with the emergence of robots and AI, has been intertwined with human history for hundreds of years, beginning with primitive machines and ideas. One of the earliest recorded automated devices was the water clock, originating in ancient Greece and utilized for time measurement. Subsequently, in the industrial revolution, machinery was created to mechanize labor in factories, resulting in heightened efficiency and output. The development of robots as we understand them now started in the middle of the 20th century. In 1954, George Devol developed the first industrial robot, known as the Unimate. It was mainly utilized in production and contributed to enhanced efficiency in the automotive sector. The word "robot" was introduced by science fiction writer Isaac Asimov, who also explored the idea of robotic ethics and the Three Laws of Robotics in his works.

1

Asimov's Three Laws of Robotics are principles that robots must adhere to in order to avoid causing any harm to humans. The regulations dictate that robots must ensure human safety as the highest priority, follow human orders unless they contradict the primary law, and safeguard their own existence unless doing so conflicts with the first or second law. The initial AI program was created in 1951 by Christopher Strachey, who designed a checkers-playing application for the Ferranti Mark I computer. Nonetheless, it was only during the 1960s and 1970s that AI research truly gained momentum, thanks to the creation of innovative algorithms and technologies like machine learning. The Dartmouth Conference in 1956 marked the academic acknowledgment of AI, as researchers convened to explore its potential and ways to progress the discipline. This conference is frequently regarded as the origin of AI as an area of research.

During the 1960s, 70s, and 80s, advancements in AI research persisted, highlighted by innovations like expert systems and the creation of Lisp, a programming language widely utilized in AI research. Nonetheless, the domain also faced challenges, like the AI winter of the 1980s, when financial support for AI research diminished because of insufficient advancements. During the 1990s, AI and automation programs started to be used for more practical purposes, including customer service chatbots and speech recognition technology. The advent of the internet also resulted in the creation of search engines and recommendation systems, which depended significantly on AI algorithms. The turn of the century ushered in additional progress in AI and automation, alongside the creation of machine learning algorithms and the emergence of big data. This resulted in the creation of autonomous vehicles, digital assistants, and tailored suggestions on websites and social platforms. Currently, automation and AI are everywhere in our everyday existence, ranging from the algorithms driving our search engines and social media feeds to the robots collaborating with us in factories and warehouses. The future of automation is expected to see increased integration with AI, featuring the advancement of sophisticated robotics, self-driving vehicles, and smart systems capable of adapting and learning independently. Though the advantages of automation are evident, there are worries regarding its effects on employment and the economy, making it crucial for society to thoughtfully explore how to utilize this technology for maximum advantage.

Importance of Autonomous Systems in Modern Society

Progress in the abilities of autonomous systems is swiftly arising due to groundbreaking achievements in creating advancements in artificial intelligence (AI). Artificial Intelligence (AI) has witnessed rapid advancements in recent years, transforming various sectors by enhancing efficiency, automating tasks, and enabling more intelligent decision-making processes (Mishra et al., 2024a, 2024b, 2024c, 2024d). Most importantly, recent findings from AI researchers across various areas are facilitating progress in developing self-learning autonomous systems—systems that can not only perceive and reason but also can self-update without human intervention. In other words, we are progressing towards systems that are capable of absorbing information from their surroundings and responding to it, while also being able to learn autonomously and modify their actions without human intervention. However, it is only recently that focus has started to shift toward the various aspects of what "learning" entails. Moreover, minimal focus has been directed towards the interconnections that these systems will encounter among natural (i.e., environment), physical (i.e., human-made), and social (i.e., areas where humans interact and operate) systems, which are perpetually evolving. Sociologists and psychologists present comprehensive theories regarding cognition, education, decision processes, legitimacy, ethics, conflict (de)escalation, and systemic interconnections that can be utilized to develop essential understanding on (1) the creation of systems; (2) their execution aimed at enhancing human advantages; and (3) how the interrelations among natural, physical, and social systems may lead to unexpected dangers of severe consequences, encompassing both deliberate and inadvertent incidents. Furthermore, addressing the challenges and opportunities that self-learning autonomous systems present leads to new avenues for inquiry in the social and behavioral sciences to enhance theories and studies related to the sciences of learning, cognition, decision-making, and systems analytics.

Autonomous systems in the world today include self-driving vehicles, which use sensors to estimate nearby obstacles and stored mapping data in order to safely navigate to a desired destination; artificial intelligence–based financial trading systems, which track market conditions and individual stocks and make independent decisions on when to buy or sell (Maney, 2017), and even new medical devices which monitor a patient's physiological condition and alter the rate of drug delivery or direct other medical intervention without caregiver input (Schwartz, 2017).

Differentiated from automated systems that operate by clear repeatable rules based on unambiguous sensed data, autonomous systems take in information about the unstructured world around them, process that information to analyze possible outcomes, and use that analysis to generate alternatives and make decisions in the face of uncertainty.

While autonomous systems hold great promise including increased access to education, public health, mobility, and transportation, there are also potential negative consequences. For example, consequences may include privacy invasions by camera vision and related tracking systems, significant opportunities for abuse and manipulation of autonomous systems such as that exhibited in the 2017 US election manipulation of social media algorithms (Woolley & Howard, 2017), and threats to personal safety as seen in the recent death of a pedestrian due to self-driving car sensor blind spots (Griggs & Wakabayashi, 2018). As a result, calls for increased government regulation of autonomous systems are growing (Laris, 2018; Lietzen, 2017).

Technology regulation typically focuses on lowering risks and reducing potential negative consequences associated with an industry, activity, or product. Technology regulation could be seen as limiting the use of a technology, which could result in a decrease in innovation and incentives to invest in newer technologies (Jaffe, Peterson, Portney, & Stavins, 1995). However, competing research demonstrates that regulation can actually drive innovation and technological progress toward societal goals (Ashford & Hall, 2012). Thus, the overarching challenge of regulating emerging technologies is to design regulations that both encourage fulfillment of a technology's potential but also manage associated risks.

There are many risks associated with autonomous systems that regulators will likely not have encountered with previous technologies, or risks will be manifested in new ways. Autonomous systems require new forms of computer-based sensing, information interpretation, and action generation in ways that are not always understood even by their own programmers (Knight, 2017). The newness and unpredictability of autonomous systems means that many failure modes will be unforeseen, and therefore untested and unmanaged. Reducing the risk of human error is often cited as a main benefit of autonomous systems (Villasenor, 2014), but that is only possible if autonomous systems become more reliable than humans.

Determining whether autonomous systems meet or exceed the reliability of humans is not straightforward due to the complexities of the software that drive these systems as well as what kind of testing is needed to make such assertions. For example, one study has asserted that in order to demonstrate a driverless car is as safe as humans, at least 275 million miles must be driven, which would take possibly up to a decade under current testing protocols (Kalra & Paddock., 2016). Thus, potentially new and different reliability assessment methods are needed if technology innovations are to be realized in more expeditious time frames. Unfortunately, testing and certification of autonomous systems is still an immature field of inquiry.

Autonomous systems rely on probabilistic reasoning and significant estimation through a mathematical estimate approach called machine learning, aka deep learning. Such pattern recognition algorithms are a data-intensive approach to developing an autonomous system world model, which serves as the core set of assumptions about who, what, and where agents in the system are and what their likely next set of behaviors and actions will be (Hutchins, Cummings, Draper, & Hughes, 2015). To date, there exists no industry consensus on how to test such systems, particularly in safety-critical environments, and such approaches to computer-based reasoning have been criticized as deeply flawed (Marcus, 2018).

Given that there are new and emerging risks that must be mitigated with the introduction of autonomous systems in safety-critical environments, it is not clear how regulatory agencies could and should respond. Regulatory agencies typically struggle to keep pace with technological change, often referred to as the pacing problem (Krisher & Billeaud, 2018). The inertia created by the procedural requirements of administrative law causes agencies and regulations to lag behind technological innovation, which is especially problematic in the current climate of rapid autonomous technology development. Institutional expertise also lags as, for example, robots and artificial intelligence are introduced into industries whose traditional regulators are unfamiliar with advanced computing and need to acquire the technical knowledge needed to understand such systems (Calo, 2014). Artificial Intelligence (AI) has transcended from being a theoretical concept to a cornerstone of technological advancement. The integration of AI across industries demonstrates it's potential to revolutionize processes, systems, and services (Mishra et al., 2024e).

In order to better understand how regulatory agencies of safety-critical systems could and should adapt as autonomous systems become more commonplace, we first discuss how such technologies come into existence from a systems engineering perspective. We then discuss how

4

three different federal regulatory agencies, the Federal Aviation Administration (FAA), the Food and Drug Administration (FDA), and the National Highway Transportation and Safety Administration (NHTSA), approach regulation of new technologies in general, and more specifically their progress with automated and autonomous systems.

Critical Components of a Robotic System

Autonomous robots are quickly changing different sectors, altering how tasks are executed. From production and supply chain to medical care and cosmic research, these smart machines are increasingly commonplace. Central to their functionality is an essential element that enables them to sense, analyze, and engage with their surroundings effortlessly. In this article, we will explore the crucial component that forms the basis for autonomous robots, enhancing their efficiency and versatility. In the rapidly advancing industrial landscape, robots and their components enhance efficiency, reduce human error, and boost productivity. Their achievement in this area can be linked to elements as straightforward as sensors and control systems, allowing industries to hold their own globally while ensuring their operations are future-ready. Robot components fundamentally make up the essential foundation of every industrial robot, ranging from simple elements of robotic arms to sophisticated mobile and industrial robots. This encompasses sensors, actuators, power sources, control mechanisms, navigation technologies, communication systems, and structural frameworks. Every single one of these is crucial to ensure that the robot operates properly and effectively when performing complex tasks. Components of robotic arms and industrial robots are crucial for overall industrial efficiency. The mobile robots are capable of navigating anywhere within their work area, allowing them to perform much of their tasks independently without the need for human assistance. The complexity and design are amplified by the blend of skills required for navigation, obstacle avoidance, and communication with staff on factory floors. The key components of a robotic arm are outlined below, along with those of mobile robots that make them beneficial in various industries.

Sensors

Sensors are the fundamental components that enable any robot to function. They are commonly referred to as a robot's eyes and ears. These elements enable the robot to observe its surroundings, detect alterations in the environment, and respond to the observed changes. In industrial robots, sensors may encompass:

- Vision Sensors: For identifying and categorizing objects.
- Proximity Sensors: These devices detect nearby objects to prevent accidents and collisions.
- Temperature and Pressure Sensors: To track conditions and modify operations accordingly.
- These sensors are vital for mobile robots, as they allow them to navigate intricate terrain, identify obstacles, and change direction based on what they detect. The effectiveness of robotic parts, like sensors, is directly related to the real-time efficiency of the robot's operation and ensures peak performance. Sensors serve as the eyes and ears for all types

of robots, gathering information through vision, hearing, tactile sensations, and/or olfactory detection. They are utilized to identify objects nearby and ascertain their position. They can likewise be utilized to recognize individuals or other nearby robots. You have various types of sensors to select from when creating your own bot:

- A GPS sensor serves as an excellent illustration of this. The GPS sensor enables the robot to determine its position on Earth, allowing it to navigate without colliding with objects or losing its way.
- Laser range finders enable your robot's computer system to monitor the distance to objects, ensuring it knows the force required for moving them (and whether any item is reachable!).
- Ultrasound sensors serve as another excellent illustration. These sensors can identify objects in their way by emitting sound waves and timing how long it takes for them to return. This data enables the robot to detect when there is an object close by that might result in harm or damage if struck by its arm or leg.

Sensors are essential elements of a robot. Without these, the robot would be incapable of knowing how to respond to its surroundings.

Actuators

Actuators are the parts that enable robots to move and interact. These 'muscles' transform electrical energy into mechanical motion, enabling robots to handle objects or navigate through their environment. Actuators are crucial in robots since, without them, robots cannot engage with their surroundings, rendering tasks unfeasible, such as material handling, welding, and assembly line processes. Actuators are the engines that drive a robot. Actuators are responsible for the movement and operation of the robot, making them a vital component. They may operate on electricity, hydraulics, or compressed air. Many robots are equipped with multiple actuators based on their requirements. The kind of actuator employed is based on the function that the robot must perform. For instance, if you desire your robot to spin in circles rapidly, you would utilize a DC motor. If you wished for your robot to raise and lower its arm continuously, then you would utilize a servo motor. If you wanted your robot to accurately position itself repeatedly, you would use a stepper motor or a brushless motor.

Here are additional kinds of actuators that are widely used parts of a robot:

- Hydraulic actuators utilize pressurized fluids to drive pistons or cylinders that activate the robot's joints or appendages. They are utilized in various industrial robots, but they aren't feasible for residential robots due to the need for costly parts and upkeep procedures.
- Pneumatic actuators operate using compressed air to drive pistons or cylinders that enable the movement of the robot's joints or limbs. They are frequently utilized in smaller robots since they consume less energy than hydraulic actuators (allowing for a more compact design).
- Electric actuators utilize electricity to activate motors that move the joints or limbs of the robot. The power can originate from batteries installed in the robot itself, or it can be obtained from an outside source like a wall plug or vehicle charger.

Power Supply

The power supply system of a robot can significantly influence how often that robot operates at its rated uptime, thereby impacting overall productivity. In the case of industrial robots, power supplies generally encompass:

- Batteries: Mobile robots require batteries that are efficient and durable, ensuring extended hours of autonomous functionality.
- Wired Energy Systems: For stationary robots, guaranteeing continuous power supply.

The effectiveness of a robot's power supply system can greatly influence its operational availability and total productivity. In high-demand industrial environments, robots need to function for long durations without failure, making power supply an essential element. Batteries are essential parts of a robot. They provide the energy source that enables robots to move and carry out tasks. It's essential to recognize that various kinds of robot batteries exist, allowing you to ensure you're using the appropriate one. The battery is the core of every robot, making it essential to choose the appropriate type for your requirement. Here are several guidelines on which type of battery will be most suitable for your project. The initial aspect to grasp is that there are two principal categories of robot batteries: primary (single-use) and secondary (rechargeable). Primary batteries such as alkaline and lithium are designed for single use, whereas secondary batteries including lead-acid, nickel-cadmium (NiCd), nickel metal hydride (NiMH), and lithium-ion can be recharged by introducing an electric current. Primary batteries are frequently utilized for small robots that have minimal energy needs; for instance, the battery could energize a toy vehicle or a remote-controlled sailboat. Secondary batteries are prevalent in bigger robots that require additional energy; for instance, they may supply power to a robotic vacuum or a forklift.

Control System

The robot's brain serves as the control system, which is central to all robots. This is the part that takes inputs from sensors and carries out commands through actuators. Control systems are frequently combined with advanced software and algorithms, enabling robots to:

- Make decisions in real-time utilizing sensor information.
- Adjust to evolving surroundings or activities.
- Manage the actions of several robotic arms or mobile units.

Programmable Logic Controller (PLC) is a dedicated digital computer utilized in automation and control systems for industrial purposes. It constantly observes sensor inputs, analyses the information, and subsequently activates outputs to manage machinery or processes in real-time. PLCs are extremely dependable and built to endure tough industrial conditions, establishing them as a norm in automation and robotics. The effectiveness of robots in industrial environments is closely linked to the control system. Accuracy, speed, and adaptability are seen to be directly related to an effective control system in an industrial environment. A high-efficiency control system has been shown to allow robots to operate independently, thus enhancing productivity and operational effectiveness. The brain is the most essential part of a robot. Without it, the robot wouldn't be capable of doing anything. It enables a robot to be intelligent and grants it the capability to perceive its environment and decide on actions to take in specific circumstances. The brain controls all functions in your robot's body, such as its limbs and sensors. Microprocessors function as the brains of robots! They provide robots with intelligence, enabling autonomy, meaning robots can operate without needing human information or instructions. Microprocessors are central to every robot and are a crucial component that enables a robot to function. They are utilized in various applications, ranging from autonomous vehicles to small toys for children. The microprocessor also manages lights and sounds, enabling the robot to interact with its surroundings and respond to us. Microprocessors are available in various forms and dimensions based on the specific tasks they are designed to perform. A well-known variant known as Arduino employs a chip referred to as Atmel AVR, which can be programmed with software called Arduino IDE (Integrated Development Environment). Another well-known type is the Raspberry Pi, which operates on Linux as its operating system, allowing it to execute different programs like Python or NodeJS.

Navigation and Mapping Technologies

For mobile robots, technologies for navigation and mapping are crucial for independent movement. These technologies, commonly known as the robots' GPS, assist robots in comprehending their surroundings and moving safely. Typical navigation systems encompass:

- LiDAR: For generating detailed maps of the robot's environment.
- SLAM (Simultaneous Localization and Mapping): An integrated process that allows the robot to create a map of its environment while concurrently determining its position accurately in real time.

By utilizing these technologies, mobile robots can navigate industrial settings autonomously, avoiding collisions and arriving at locations without human intervention. This ability greatly enhances operational efficiency as workflows take place continuously, allowing the machines to operate autonomously.

Communication Systems

Communication systems enable robots to engage with other machines, human operators, and centralized control systems. These systems utilize technologies such as:

- Wi-Fi and Bluetooth: To facilitate interaction between the robots and the central control units without needing a physical link.
- Machine-to-Machine Communication (M2M): This allows robots to operate in a synchronized manner as they strive to achieve their goals.

Aside from that, effective communication systems will be crucial for its operation as numerous robots or human employees need to share or obtain information from each other in these environments. Communication serves as another vital element of a robot. It enables you to link to the robot, customize its tasks, and manage it remotely.

Various forms of communication exist:

Cables transmit information between two devices at a physical level, like USB cables or network cables. They are typically employed to establish connections among computers, peripherals, and additional devices.

Bluetooth - This wireless protocol operates over short distances, employing radio waves to link devices. It's incredibly quick and allows you to link to multiple devices at the same time.

WiFi - WiFi resembles Bluetooth, yet it employs radio waves rather than infrared light to communicate. It also allows you to link several devices simultaneously, but it offers a greater range than Bluetooth (approximately 300 feet).

Infrared - Infrared is yet another short-range communication technique that utilizes light waves rather than radio waves or sound waves (like auditory waves).

Chassis and Structural Components

The chassis and structural elements offer stability and support for the robot's functioning components. These elements constitute the basis of the robot, providing resilience and robustness, particularly in challenging industrial settings. The design structure of robots influences:

- Load-bearing ability: Crucial for robots managing hefty items.
- Adaptability: Enabling robots to function in different environments and situations.

Drive Train

The drive train is the robot's part responsible for its movement, and it can be one of various types. A chain drive is an excellent option for robots that must navigate uneven surfaces or work in areas with obstacles present. The chain is capable of encircling items in its way and continues progressing if needed, while still enabling the robot to pivot effortlessly. A wheeled drive train is favored as it is user-friendly and straightforward to begin with. Wheels are beneficial for relocating your robot across extensive distances or uneven ground. Numerous other varieties of drive trains exist based on your requirements, but these two selections rank among the most favored options for warehouses and various industrial locations where the environment may pose challenges to a robot's mobility.

End Effectors

Although the body is usually the most apparent section of a robot, end effectors can be considered one of the most crucial components of robots. They enable robots to engage with their surroundings. For instance, if you desire a robot to grasp an item and relocate it to another location (assuming its hands are capable of movement), then you require an end effector to perform this task on your behalf. There exist various kinds of end effectors:

Hands: A hand is capable of holding objects and relocating them. It's excellent for grabbing tiny items such as pens or cups!

Grippers: A gripper features several fingers that can be opened or closed to securely hold objects better than a single finger could achieve. This is beneficial when raising heavy items such as boxes or stones from dirt holes (and possibly relocating them to different holes as well).

Suction cup: A suction cup adheres to surfaces to prevent falling when carrying heavy objects (such as the previously referenced rocks).

Program

A robotics program is not a tangible part. Nonetheless, it remains an essential component of the entire. Every basic part of the robots we've examined receives stimuli or provides feedback. The software within a robot provides the common sense that motivates those actions. When you consider it, a program resembles the essence of a robot. It's what provides them with their character and their distinctive voice. It defines their identity and enables them to perform their actions. However, in contrast to humans, robots lack free will. They don't decide independently—that's the purpose of programming! A program determines how a robot will act in specific situations. And if you've owned a pet that appeared to have its own personality (and perhaps even some peculiarities), it's due to them being simply wired differently than other animals. Certain pets are reserved and subdued, while others are friendly and energetic—it entirely relies on the programming that was implemented in them when they were initially created.

The essential aspect of autonomous robots is the seamless incorporation of sensing technologies, processing units, actuators, connectivity, power sources, safety features, navigation, machine learning, human-robot collaboration, and self-repair functions. This collaboration enables these smart machines to execute various tasks independently, with accuracy, efficiency, and flexibility.

Fundamental Concepts in Robotics

Robotics is a field of engineering and science that encompasses electronics engineering, mechanical engineering, computer science, among others. This field focuses on the design, building, and operation of robots, sensory feedback, and processing of information. These are various technologies that are set to take over human roles and activities in the years ahead. These robots are intended for a variety of uses, yet they are often employed in delicate situations such as bomb detection and the deactivation of different explosive devices. Robots can adopt various shapes, but many of them are designed to resemble humans. Robots that resemble humans might be able to walk, speak, think, and perform all the functions a human can undertake. The majority of today's robots takes inspiration from nature and is referred to as bio-inspired robots. Robotics is the field of engineering focused on the conception, design, operation, and production of robots. An author named Isaac Asimov claimed he was the first to use the term "robotics" in a short story written in the 1940s. In that narrative, Issac proposed three rules for directing such robotic machines. Eventually, these three principles were labeled as Isaac's three laws of Robotics. These three regulations assert that:

- Robots will never pose a threat to humans.
- Robots will adhere to commands provided by humans without violating the law.
- Robots will safeguard themselves while adhering to other regulations.

Kinematics and Dynamics of Robots

Robotics is an interdisciplinary field that blends mechanical engineering, electrical engineering, and computer science. The kinematics and dynamics of robots form the foundation for analyzing and designing robotic systems. Understanding these principles is crucial for applications in industrial automation, autonomous vehicles, medical robotics, and space exploration. Kinematics deals with the motion of robots without considering the forces and torques that cause the motion. It is divided into two primary categories:

- Forward Kinematics (FK)

- Inverse Kinematics (IK)

Forward Kinematics (FK)

Forward kinematics involves computing the position and orientation of a robot's end-effector given the joint parameters (angles or displacements).

Inverse Kinematics (IK)

Inverse kinematics finds the joint variables that achieve a desired end-effector position and orientation. This is more complex than forward kinematics due to the nonlinearity of the equations.

Robot dynamics considers the forces and torques required to produce motion. It is crucial for control, stability, and motion planning.

Applications of Kinematics and Dynamics in Robotics

- Industrial Robotics – Used in manufacturing for pick-and-place, welding, and painting.
- Humanoid Robotics – Helps in designing bipedal walking and dexterous manipulation.
- Medical Robotics – Used in surgical robots (e.g., Da Vinci system).
- Autonomous Vehicles – Self-driving cars use dynamic models for motion planning.
- Space Robotics – Used in robotic arms on satellites and planetary rovers.
- The study of kinematics and dynamics is crucial for developing efficient robotic systems. Kinematics helps in understanding motion, while dynamics ensures control and stability. Advances in AI, optimization, and control techniques are pushing robotics towards more intelligent and autonomous behavior.

Sensors and Perception Systems in Robotics

In robotics, sensors and perception systems are fundamental components that enable robots to interpret and interact with their environment. These systems allow robots to gather data, process information, and make informed decisions, thereby facilitating autonomy and adaptability in various applications. Robotic sensors are devices that detect changes in the environment or the robot's internal state, converting physical stimuli into signals that can be measured and analyzed. These sensors are categorized based on the type of data they collect:

- Proprioceptive Sensors: Measure internal parameters of the robot, such as joint angles, motor speeds, and battery levels. Examples include encoders, gyroscopes, and accelerometers.
- Exteroceptive Sensors: Gather information from the robot's external environment. Examples include cameras, LiDAR, sonar, and tactile sensors.

Types of Exteroceptive Sensors

Vision Sensors

- Cameras: Capture images or video, enabling object recognition, tracking, and navigation.
- Stereo Cameras: Utilize two lenses to obtain depth information, aiding in 3D perception.
- **LiDAR (Light Detection and Ranging)**
- Uses laser beams to measure distances to objects, creating precise 3D maps of the environment.

- **Sonar Sensors**
- Employ sound waves to detect objects and measure distances, commonly used in underwater robotics.
- **Tactile Sensors**
- Mimic the sense of touch, allowing robots to detect contact, pressure, and texture.

Perception Systems in Robotics

Perception systems integrate data from multiple sensors to construct a coherent understanding of the robot's surroundings. This process involves several key components:

Sensor Fusion

Combines data from various sensors to enhance accuracy and reliability. For instance, merging LiDAR and camera data can improve object detection and environmental mapping.

Environmental Mapping

Generates maps of the robot's surroundings, essential for navigation and obstacle avoidance. Techniques like Simultaneous Localization and Mapping (SLAM) are commonly employed.

Object Recognition and Tracking

Identifies and monitors objects within the environment, enabling tasks like sorting, manipulation, and interaction.

Localization

Determines the robot's position within a known map, crucial for path planning and autonomous navigation.

Challenges in Robotic Perception

Despite advancements, robotic perception faces several challenges:

- Sensor Limitations: Factors such as limited resolution, range, and susceptibility to environmental conditions can affect performance.
- Data Processing: Handling and interpreting large volumes of sensor data in real-time requires significant computational resources.
- Dynamic Environments: Adapting to changing conditions and unpredictable obstacles remains a complex problem.
- Sensor Placement Optimization: Determining the optimal number and arrangement of sensors on a robot to maximize perception capabilities is a critical design consideration. Research has shown that sensor placement significantly influences the accuracy of tasks like Simultaneous Localization and Mapping (SLAM).

Recent Advancements

The field of robotic perception is continually evolving, with recent developments including:

- Advanced Sensor Technologies: Innovations such as pre-touch distance ranging and material detection sensors enhance robotic grasping capabilities by providing detailed information about object proximity and composition.
- Enhanced Sensor Fusion Techniques: Combining data from multiple sensors, such as vision and radar, improves environmental perception and object detection, leading to more robust and reliable robotic systems.

- Improved Real-Time Processing Frameworks: Developments in hardware-software integration frameworks enable real-time processing of sensor data, facilitating tasks like navigation, object detection, and manipulation without the need for dedicated high-power computing resources.

Applications of Sensors and Perception Systems

Robotic sensors and perception systems are integral to various applications:

- Industrial Automation: Robots equipped with advanced perception systems perform tasks such as assembly, inspection, and packaging with high precision.
- Autonomous Vehicles: Utilize a combination of cameras, LiDAR, and radar to navigate complex environments safely.
- Healthcare Robotics: Assist in surgeries and patient care by providing precise movements and environmental awareness.
- Agricultural Robotics: Employ sensors to monitor crop health, soil conditions, and automate harvesting processes.

Sensors and perception systems are the cornerstone of robotic autonomy, enabling machines to interpret and interact with their environment effectively. Ongoing research and technological advancements continue to enhance these systems, expanding the capabilities and applications of robots across various industries.

Motion Planning and Navigation

Motion planning and navigation are critical aspects of robotics, enabling autonomous robots to move safely and efficiently through their environments. These concepts are fundamental for applications such as autonomous vehicles, robotic arms, mobile robots, and drones.

Motion Planning: Definition and Importance

Motion planning involves computing a path from an initial position to a goal position while avoiding obstacles. It is widely used in:

- Autonomous Vehicles: Planning collision-free routes in dynamic environments.
- Industrial Robots: Ensuring safe movement of robotic arms.
- Drones and UAVs: Navigating through complex 3D spaces.
- Medical Robotics: Guiding surgical instruments with high precision.
- Mathematically, motion planning is formulated as a path finding problem in configuration space (C-space), where:
- Configuration: A unique state of the robot (e.g., joint angles for manipulators, position for mobile robots).
- C-space: A high-dimensional space representing all possible configurations.
- Obstacles: Defined as regions in C-space where movement is not allowed.

Types of Motion Planning Algorithms

Classical Motion Planning Approaches

Graph-Based Algorithms

- Dijkstra's Algorithm: Finds the shortest path but is computationally expensive.
- A: An improved version of Dijkstra that incorporates heuristics for faster path finding.

- D-Algorithm: A dynamic version of A used in changing environments.

Sampling-Based Algorithms
1. Used for high-dimensional spaces where traditional methods are inefficient.
2. Rapidly-exploring Random Trees (RRT)
3. Efficient for navigating complex environments.
4. Constructs a tree by randomly sampling points in the C-space.
5. Probabilistic Roadmaps (PRM)
6. Constructs a network of valid paths and searches for an optimal route.

Potential Field Methods
1. Treats obstacles as repulsive forces and the goal as an attractive force.
2. Useful for real-time applications but may get stuck in local minima.

Modern Motion Planning Techniques

Optimization-Based Approaches
- Trajectory Optimization (e.g., CHOMP, STOMP, and GPMP)
- Uses gradient-based optimization for smooth paths.
- Model Predictive Control (MPC)
- Continuously optimizes motion over a finite time horizon.

Machine Learning and AI-Based Approaches
- Deep Reinforcement Learning (DRL)
- Trains robots to navigate by trial and error.
- Neural Motion Planning (NMP)
- Uses deep learning to predict feasible paths in complex environments.

Hybrid Approaches
- Combine sampling, optimization, and AI for robust planning.
- Example: Hybrid A Algorithm (used in autonomous vehicle navigation).

Navigation in Robotics
Navigation refers to the ability of a robot to move from one location to another while understanding and interacting with its surroundings. This requires three fundamental components:
- Localization – Determining the robot's position.
- Mapping – Creating a map of the environment.
- Path Execution – Following the planned path using motion control.

Localization Techniques
Localization helps the robot determine where it is in an environment. It is categorized into:
- Relative Localization (Odometry): Uses wheel encoders and IMUs to estimate movement.
- Absolute Localization: Uses external references like GPS, LiDAR, and vision-based SLAM.
- Simultaneous Localization and Mapping (SLAM): A technique where a robot maps an environment while localizing itself within it.

Popular SLAM Algorithms:

- EKF-SLAM (Extended Kalman Filter SLAM)
- FastSLAM
- ORB-SLAM (Vision-based SLAM)

Mapping and Environmental Representation

Mapping allows a robot to understand its environment. Common mapping techniques include:

- Grid-Based Maps (Occupancy Grid): Discretizes space into cells (e.g., used in ROS Navigation Stack).
- Topological Maps: Represents the environment as a graph of connected locations.
- Semantic Maps: Includes object recognition and contextual understanding.

Path Execution and Control

Once a path is planned, the robot must execute it using control systems. Common approaches:

- Proportional-Integral-Derivative (PID) Control: A simple and effective method for trajectory tracking.
- Pure Pursuit Algorithm: Used for mobile robot path tracking.
- Dynamic Window Approach (DWA): Helps avoid obstacles dynamically.

Challenges in Motion Planning and Navigation

- Uncertain Environments – Robots must adapt to dynamic and unpredictable surroundings.
- High-Dimensional Planning – Complex robots (e.g., humanoids) require sophisticated planning in multiple degrees of freedom (DOF).
- Real-Time Constraints – Autonomous systems must compute plans quickly to function effectively.
- Sensor Limitations – Noisy and imperfect sensor data can degrade localization accuracy.

Applications of Motion Planning and Navigation

- Autonomous Vehicles – Uses LiDAR, cameras, and AI for self-driving capabilities.
- Drones – Requires 3D motion planning for obstacle avoidance in aerial navigation.
- Warehouse Robots – Navigate autonomously using mapping and localization (e.g., Amazon Kiva Robots).
- Medical Robotics – Uses precise path planning for minimally invasive surgeries.
- Space Exploration – Mars rovers use motion planning for navigation on alien terrain.

Motion planning and navigation are essential for robotics, enabling autonomous decision-making in diverse environments. With advancements in AI, optimization, and sensor technologies, robotic navigation continues to improve in accuracy, efficiency, and adaptability.

Control Systems in Robotics

Control systems are fundamental to robotics, enabling machines to perform tasks with precision, adaptability, and autonomy. They govern the behavior of robots, ensuring desired outputs in response to specific inputs, and are integral to applications ranging from industrial automation to autonomous vehicles. A control system in robotics manages commands, directs, or regulates the behavior of devices or systems to achieve desired results. It comprises hardware and software components that work in unison to control the robot's movements and operations.

Components

- Controller: The brain of the robot, processing inputs and determining appropriate outputs.
- Actuators: Devices that execute movements, such as motors or hydraulic systems.
- Sensors: Provide feedback by measuring various parameters like position, speed, and environmental factors.
- Feedback Mechanism: Ensures the system can adjust its actions based on sensor data to achieve desired performance.

Types of Control Systems

Open-Loop Control Systems

In open-loop systems, the controller sends commands to the actuators without receiving feedback. These systems are simpler but lack the ability to correct errors or adapt to changes. Example: A simple timed motor operation where the motor runs for a set duration regardless of its actual position.

Closed-Loop (Feedback) Control Systems

Closed-loop systems utilize feedback from sensors to adjust actions continually, enhancing accuracy and adaptability. Example: A thermostat-controlled heating system that adjusts heating based on the current temperature.

Control Strategies in Robotics

Proportional-Integral-Derivative (PID) Control

PID controllers are widely used due to their simplicity and effectiveness. They adjust the control input based on the error, its integral, and its derivative.

- Proportional (P): Responds to the current error magnitude.
- Integral (I): Accounts for the accumulation of past errors.
- Derivative (D): Predicts future error based on its rate of change.

The combination of these three actions provides a control signal that can adjust the system promptly and accurately.

Adaptive Control

Adaptive control systems modify their parameters in real-time to cope with changes in system dynamics or the environment. This is crucial for robots operating in unpredictable settings. Application: Robots performing tasks with varying payloads, where the control system adjusts to maintain performance.

Optimal Control

Optimal control aims to determine control inputs that minimize or maximize a certain performance criterion, such as energy consumption or time. Example: Trajectory optimization in robotic arms to achieve movements that consume the least energy.

Robust Control

Robust control deals with systems that have uncertainties, ensuring performance remains satisfactory despite variations. Application: Autonomous drones maintaining stability in varying wind conditions.

Advanced Topics in Robotic Control

Model Predictive Control (MPC)

MPC involves solving an optimization problem at each time step, using a model of the system to predict future behavior and optimize performance over a finite horizon. Application: Self-driving cars planning optimal paths while considering dynamic obstacles.

Learning-Based Control

With advancements in artificial intelligence, robots can now learn control strategies from data. Techniques like reinforcement learning enable robots to improve performance through trial and error. Example: Robots learning to navigate complex terrains by interacting with the environment.

Hybrid Control Systems

Hybrid control combines different control strategies to leverage their respective strengths. For instance, combining PID control with adaptive elements can enhance performance in systems with both predictable and unpredictable dynamics.

Challenges and Future Directions

- Real-Time Processing: Ensuring control systems can process sensor data and compute responses rapidly is critical for applications like autonomous driving.
- Scalability: Developing control algorithms that perform well in high-dimensional systems, such as humanoid robots with many joints.
- Safety and Reliability: As robots are increasingly used in human environments, ensuring their actions are safe and reliable is paramount.
- Integration with AI: Combining traditional control systems with AI techniques to enhance decision-making and adaptability.

Control systems are the backbone of robotic functionality, enabling machines to perform tasks with precision and adaptability. Ongoing research and technological advancements continue to enhance these systems, expanding the capabilities and applications of robots across various industries.

Autonomous Systems and Their Applications

Autonomous systems are machines or software that can perform tasks with minimal or no human intervention. These systems leverage artificial intelligence (AI), machine learning, control theory, and advanced sensing technologies to make decisions in real time. An autonomous system is a self-governing entity capable of perceiving its environment, making decisions, and executing actions to achieve specific goals. These systems can operate in diverse fields such as robotics, transportation, healthcare, and defense.

Autonomous systems typically consist of:

- Perception Systems – Sensors such as LiDAR, cameras, and IMUs for real-time data acquisition.
- Decision-Making Algorithms – AI-driven logic for planning and adapting to changing conditions.
- Control Systems – Mechanisms that ensure precise execution of planned actions.
- Communication Networks – Enables coordination in multi-agent systems (e.g., swarm robotics).

Types of Autonomous Systems

Autonomous Vehicles

Autonomous vehicles (AVs) include self-driving cars, autonomous drones, and unmanned ground vehicles (UGVs).

- Self-Driving Cars (Autonomous Cars)
- Uses LiDAR, radar, and deep learning models for perception.
- Examples: Tesla Autopilot, Waymo, and Cruise AVs.
- Applications: Public transport, logistics, and ride-sharing.
- Autonomous Drones (UAVs - Unmanned Aerial Vehicles)
- Used for surveillance, delivery, and search-and-rescue missions.
- Examples: Amazon Prime Air, DJI drones, and military UAVs.

Industrial Automation and Robotics

Autonomous robots are revolutionizing manufacturing, logistics, and service industries.

- Warehouse and Logistics Robots
- Used for inventory management and order fulfillment.
- Example: Amazon Kiva Robots.
- Autonomous Mobile Robots (AMRs)
- Navigate warehouses using SLAM and AI.
- Example: Boston Dynamics' Stretch.

Healthcare and Medical Robotics

Autonomous systems enhance diagnostics, surgery, and elderly care.

- Surgical Robots
- Perform minimally invasive procedures with high precision.
- Example: Da Vinci Surgical System.
- Autonomous Patient Monitoring
- AI-powered systems track patient vitals and predict health risks.

Defense and Military Applications

Autonomous systems are widely used in surveillance, reconnaissance, and unmanned combat.

- Unmanned Combat Aerial Vehicles (UCAVs)
- Example: MQ-9 Reaper drone.
- Autonomous Underwater Vehicles (AUVs)
- Used for naval defense and deep-sea exploration.

Smart Cities and Infrastructure

Autonomous systems contribute to efficient urban management.

- Autonomous Public Transport – Self-driving buses and trains.
- AI-Driven Traffic Management – Adaptive traffic lights reduce congestion.
- Smart Grid Systems – AI-based power distribution networks.

Space Exploration

Autonomous systems are essential for space missions where human intervention is limited.

- Mars Rovers (e.g., Perseverance, Curiosity) – Navigate and conduct experiments autonomously.
- Autonomous Satellites – Manage Earth observation and communication networks.

Healthcare Applications

Autonomous Surgical Systems

Robotic-assisted surgeries have become increasingly prevalent, offering precision and minimally invasive procedures. Systems like the Da Vinci Surgical System enable surgeons to perform complex operations with enhanced dexterity and control.

Remote and Autonomous Medical Care

In scenarios where immediate medical expertise is unavailable, autonomous systems provide critical support. For instance, NASA has explored in-flight autonomous medical care for long-duration space missions, enabling crew members to manage health issues with minimal real-time support from Earth.

AI-Driven Diagnostics

Artificial intelligence enhances diagnostic accuracy by analyzing medical data to identify patterns indicative of specific conditions. AI-based virtual assistants can offer medical advice to field medics, improving decision-making in critical situations.

Defense Applications

Unmanned Aerial Vehicles (UAVs)

Autonomous drones are integral to modern military operations, conducting surveillance, reconnaissance, and combat missions without endangering human pilots. Advancements in AI have led to drones capable of independent decision-making in dynamic environments.

Underwater Autonomous Systems

The development of autonomous underwater drones, such as the Ghost Shark and Manta Ray, has expanded capabilities in maritime defense. These drones can operate at significant depths for extended periods, performing tasks like intelligence gathering and infrastructure protection.

AI in Defense Technology

The integration of AI into defense systems enhances battlefield awareness and decision-making. The European Commission has significantly increased funding for military-related research, focusing on projects like drones, radar systems, and counter-hypersonic missile defenses.

Space Exploration Applications
Autonomous Spacecraft and Rovers
Autonomous systems are essential for space missions where real-time human control is impractical. Rovers like NASA's Perseverance navigate and conduct experiments on Mars autonomously, adapting to unexpected challenges without direct intervention.
AI-Powered Satellite Surveillance
Companies like Anduril are expanding into the space sector by deploying AI-powered systems for space situational awareness and missile tracking. Partnering with startups like Apex, they aim to enhance the capabilities of satellite hardware for defense applications.
Autonomous Medical Support in Space
Long-duration space missions necessitate autonomous medical systems capable of providing care with minimal Earth-based support. NASA's research into autonomous medical care aims to equip crew members with the tools and knowledge to manage health issues independently during missions. The continuous advancement of autonomous systems is transforming multiple sectors, offering solutions that enhance operational efficiency, safety, and capabilities. As technology progresses, the integration of AI and autonomous systems is poised to address increasingly complex challenges across various domains.
Challenges in Autonomous Systems
- Safety and Reliability – Ensuring robustness in unpredictable environments.
- Ethical and Legal Concerns – Addressing liability and decision-making biases.
- Cyber security Risks – Preventing hacking and malicious interference.
- Scalability – Adapting autonomous solutions for widespread deployment.
Future Trends and Innovations
- Advances in AI and Deep Learning – Enhancing decision-making accuracy.
- 5G and Edge Computing – Enabling real-time processing for distributed autonomous networks.
- Human-Robot Collaboration – Increasing integration of autonomous systems with human workers.
Autonomous systems are revolutionizing various sectors by enhancing efficiency, safety, and capabilities. This discussion delves into their applications in healthcare, defense, and space exploration, supported by recent developments and references.
AI and Machine Learning in Robotics
Artificial Intelligence (AI) and Machine Learning (ML) are revolutionizing robotics, enabling autonomous decision-making, adaptability, and enhanced perception. These technologies allow robots to learn from experience, optimize performance, and interact seamlessly with dynamic environments.
Role of AI in Robotics
AI enables robots to:
- Perceive their surroundings using sensors and vision systems.
- Learn from data and experiences to improve over time.

- Make decisions autonomously, minimizing human intervention.
- Interact with humans and other machines using natural language and gestures.

Machine Learning Techniques in Robotics

Supervised Learning
- Robots learn from labeled datasets where input-output mappings are provided.
- Example: Image recognition for object detection in warehouse automation.

Unsupervised Learning
- Robots identify patterns in unlabeled data.
- Example: Clustering different objects in an environment for autonomous navigation.

Reinforcement Learning (RL)
- Robots learn through trial and error by maximizing rewards in a given environment.
- Example: Boston Dynamics' quadruped robot, Spot, improving walking strategies through RL.

Deep Learning (DL)
- Neural networks process large datasets for complex decision-making.
- Example: Self-driving cars using convolutional neural networks (CNNs) for real-time perception.

AI Applications in Robotics

Computer Vision for Perception
- AI-driven image processing helps robots detect objects, recognize faces, and navigate environments.
- Example: Amazon's fulfillment robots use vision-based AI to identify and sort packages.

Natural Language Processing (NLP) for Human-Robot Interaction
- AI enables robots to understand and respond to spoken commands.
- Example: Social robots like Pepper and Sophia use NLP for customer interactions.

Motion Planning and Control
- AI optimizes robot movements for efficiency and precision.
- Example: Autonomous drones dynamically adjust flight paths to avoid obstacles.

Predictive Maintenance in Industrial Robotics
- Machine learning models predict failures before they occur, reducing downtime.
- Example: AI-driven predictive analytics in automotive manufacturing lines.

Challenges in AI-Powered Robotics
- Data Requirements – AI models require large amounts of high-quality training data.
- Real-Time Processing – Decision-making must be fast and reliable.
- Ethical Concerns – AI in robotics raises issues related to privacy and job displacement.
- Generalization – Robots trained in controlled environments must adapt to unpredictable real-world conditions.

Future Trends and Innovations
- Edge AI – On-device processing for real-time decision-making.

- AI and Robotics in Healthcare – AI-assisted robotic surgery and eldercare robots.
- Swarm Robotics – Multiple AI-powered robots collaborating for complex tasks.
- Self-Learning Robots – AI models capable of continuous adaptation without human intervention.

Artificial Intelligence (AI) and Machine Learning (ML) are pivotal in advancing robotics, enabling machines to perform complex tasks with increasing autonomy and efficiency. Recent developments across various industries highlight the transformative impact of AI and ML in robotics.

Recent Developments in AI and ML in Robotics

Agricultural Robotics

Swarm Farm Robotics has inaugurated a manufacturing hub in Australia's Darling Downs, focusing on autonomous farm robots. These modular machines, equipped with cameras and sensors, are designed for tasks such as planting, weeding, and harvesting, aiming to revolutionize modern agriculture. The facility also offers high-tech employment opportunities in engineering and software development.

AI-Driven Humanoid Robots

Meta Platforms is venturing into the development of AI-powered humanoid robots intended for physical tasks. Utilizing their AI models, known as Llama, Meta aims to create consumer humanoid robots capable of performing various functions, marking a significant step in AI and robotics integration.

Industrial Automation

Amazon has integrated over 750,000 robots within its fulfillment centers to enhance operational efficiency. These robots, including fully autonomous units like Proteus and AI-equipped robotic arms such as Sparrow, are utilized for transporting packages, sorting items, and creating customized packaging, thereby streamlining warehouse operations.

Applications of AI and ML in Robotics

Autonomous Navigation

AI enables robots to navigate complex environments independently by processing data from various sensors and employing machine learning algorithms to make real-time decisions. This capability is crucial in applications ranging from self-driving vehicles to drones and warehouse automation.

Object Recognition and Manipulation

Machine learning algorithms enhance a robot's ability to recognize and handle objects, improving performance in tasks such as sorting, assembly, and packaging. For instance, AI-driven computer vision systems allow robots to identify and manipulate items with precision, which is essential in manufacturing and logistics.

Human-Robot Interaction

AI facilitates more natural interactions between humans and robots through advancements in natural language processing and adaptive learning. This leads to improved collaboration in settings like healthcare, customer service, and domestic assistance, where robots can understand and respond to human commands effectively.

Predictive Maintenance

In industrial settings, AI and ML are employed to predict equipment failures before they occur, allowing for proactive maintenance. This approach reduces downtime and maintenance costs by analyzing data from sensors to identify patterns indicative of potential issues.

Challenges and Future Directions

Data Requirements

Developing effective AI models necessitates large datasets for training. Ensuring the availability of high-quality, labeled data remains a significant challenge in many applications.

Real-Time Processing

Robotic systems must process information and make decisions rapidly. Achieving the necessary computational speed and efficiency, particularly in resource-constrained environments, is an ongoing area of research.

Ethical and Social Implications

The integration of AI in robotics raises questions about job displacement, privacy, and the ethical use of autonomous systems. Addressing these concerns requires careful consideration and the development of appropriate policies and guidelines.

The fusion of AI and ML with robotics is driving significant advancements across various sectors, from agriculture to industrial automation. As these technologies continue to evolve, they promise to enhance the capabilities of robotic systems, making them more intelligent, efficient, and adaptable to complex tasks. - Deep Learning for Perception and Decision-Making

Swarm Robotics and Multi-Agent Systems

Swarm robotics and multi-agent systems (MAS) represent advanced paradigms in robotics where multiple autonomous agents collaborate to achieve complex tasks efficiently. Inspired by biological swarms, these systems emphasize decentralized control, scalability, and robustness. Swarm robotics is a field that studies the coordination of large groups of relatively simple robots to perform tasks that are difficult for individual robots. These systems draw inspiration from natural swarms such as ants, bees, and birds.

Multi-Agent Systems (MAS)

Multi-Agent Systems refers to a collection of autonomous agents interacting within an environment to achieve shared or individual goals. Unlike swarm robotics, which often involves homogeneous agents, MAS can consist of heterogeneous agents with specialized roles.

Characteristics of Swarm Robotics and MAS

Feature	Swarm Robotics	Multi-Agent Systems
Decentralization	Fully decentralized	Can be centralized or decentralized
Scalability	Highly scalable	Moderately scalable
Robustness	High fault tolerance	Depends on coordination strategy
Communication	Local interactions (e.g., stigmergy)	Direct or indirect communication
Heterogeneity	Mostly homogeneous agents	Often heterogeneous agents

Techniques and Algorithms
Swarm Intelligence Algorithms
Swarm intelligence refers to the collective behavior of decentralized, self-organized systems. Common algorithms include:

- Particle Swarm Optimization (PSO) – Inspired by bird flocking, used for optimization tasks.
- Ant Colony Optimization (ACO) – Based on ant foraging behavior, used in path finding and routing problems.
- Artificial Bee Colony (ABC) Algorithm – Simulates bee foraging for optimization in robotic exploration.

Distributed Decision-Making
- Consensus Algorithms – Ensure agreement among agents (e.g., flocking, formation control).
- Reinforcement Learning (RL) – Enables agents to learn optimal behaviors through trial and error.

Communication Methods
- Explicit Communication – Robots exchange data via wireless networks.
- Implicit Communication (Stigmergy) – Agents leave signals in the environment (e.g., pheromones in ants).

Applications of Swarm Robotics and MAS
Search and Rescue Operations
Swarm robots are deployed in disaster zones to locate survivors and map hazardous areas. Example: Aerial drone swarms used in earthquake-affected regions.

Environmental Monitoring
Swarm robots monitor air and water quality, track pollution, and survey wildlife habitats. Example: Robot fish for detecting water contamination.

Military and Defense
Autonomous drone swarms perform surveillance, reconnaissance, and coordinated attacks. Example: The US military's Perdix drone swarm project.

Agriculture and Precision Farming
Swarm robots are used for planting, watering, and harvesting crops efficiently. Example: Swarm Farm Robotics' autonomous farming solutions.

Space Exploration
NASA explores using swarm robots for planetary exploration and asteroid mining. Example: Autonomous robotic swarms for lunar surface mapping.

Challenges in Swarm Robotics and MAS
- Scalability – Ensuring coordination in large-scale systems.
- Communication Constraints – Managing decentralized networks with limited bandwidth.
- Energy Efficiency – Prolonging the operational time of swarm robots.
- Security Risks – Preventing adversarial attacks in multi-agent interactions.

Future Trends and Innovations

- AI-Driven Swarm Intelligence – Enhancing decision-making with deep learning.
- Bio-Inspired Swarm Robotics – Developing robots that mimic biological organisms.
- Quantum Swarm Computing – Leveraging quantum algorithms for faster coordination.
- Human-Swarm Interaction – Enabling intuitive human control over robotic swarms.

Swarm robotics and multi-agent systems (MAS) are transformative fields in robotics, enabling autonomous agents to collaborate and perform complex tasks efficiently. These systems draw inspiration from natural phenomena, such as the coordinated behavior of ants and bees, to achieve objectives that individual agents might find challenging.

Applications of Swarm Robotics

1. Environmental Monitoring: Swarm robots are deployed to collect data on air quality, water quality, and oceanographic conditions. Their collective sensing capabilities allow for comprehensive environmental assessments.
2. Search and Rescue Operations: In disaster scenarios, swarm robots can navigate hazardous environments to locate survivors, map affected areas, and deliver essential supplies, thereby enhancing rescue efforts. Agriculture: Swarm robotics facilitates tasks such as planting, watering, and harvesting crops. The collaborative nature of these robots enables efficient and precise agricultural operations.
3. Manufacturing: In industrial settings, swarm robots can autonomously assemble products, manage inventory, and perform quality control, leading to increased efficiency and reduced human labor.

Applications of Multi-Agent Systems

1. Healthcare: MAS enhance diagnostics, patient monitoring, and data analysis, leading to more efficient and effective medical services.
2. Smart Grids: MAS manage electricity distribution by coordinating generators, storage, utilities, and consumers, facilitating the integration of renewable energy sources and improving grid reliability.
3. Disaster Response: Autonomous robot agents cooperate to map disaster sites, locate survivors, and provide critical supplies, improving the effectiveness of emergency response efforts.
4. Supply Chain Management: MAS optimize logistics, inventory management, and distribution processes, enhancing efficiency and reducing operational costs in supply chains.
5. The integration of swarm robotics and multi-agent systems is advancing various sectors by enabling autonomous, efficient, and scalable solutions to complex problems.

Robotics in Industry 4.0

Industry 4.0, often referred to as the Fourth Industrial Revolution, represents a paradigm shift in industrial automation, integrating advanced digital technologies such as the Internet of Things (IoT), Artificial Intelligence (AI), cloud computing, big data analytics, and robotics. Robotics plays a crucial role in transforming modern industries by enabling intelligent, autonomous, and highly efficient production systems. Unlike traditional automation, which primarily focuses on repetitive and pre-programmed tasks, Industry 4.0 robots are equipped with AI, real-time data processing, and machine learning capabilities, allowing them to adapt to dynamic environments, make independent decisions, and collaborate with human workers. This transition to smart manufacturing enhances productivity, reduces operational costs, minimizes errors, and significantly improves overall production efficiency.

One of the most significant advancements in Industry 4.0 robotics is the integration of collaborative robots (cobots) that work alongside human operators to enhance precision, safety, and efficiency in production lines. Cobots are designed to perform tasks such as assembly, material handling, and quality inspection while ensuring seamless human-robot interaction through sensors and AI-driven vision systems. Unlike traditional industrial robots that operate in isolated environments, cobots are inherently flexible and can be reprogrammed for multiple tasks, making them ideal for small-batch manufacturing and customized production. Companies like Universal Robots and Fanuc have pioneered cobot technology, enabling industries such as automotive, electronics, and pharmaceuticals to enhance their manufacturing capabilities.

Another critical application of robotics in Industry 4.0 is autonomous mobile robots (AMRs) and automated guided vehicles (AGVs), which streamline logistics, inventory management, and warehouse operations. AMRs leverage AI and IoT to navigate factory floors autonomously, optimize material transportation, and coordinate with other robotic systems in real time. Unlike traditional AGVs, which follow fixed pathways, AMRs use advanced perception technologies such as LiDAR, computer vision, and machine learning to adapt to dynamic environments, avoid obstacles, and optimize their movement paths. Companies like Amazon Robotics, KUKA, and Boston Dynamics have revolutionized supply chain and warehouse automation by deploying fleets of AMRs capable of performing tasks such as order picking, sorting, and delivery with minimal human intervention.

One of the most groundbreaking innovations in Industry 4.0 robotics is the concept of cyber-physical systems (CPS) and digital twins, where physical robots are connected to cloud-based digital replicas for real-time monitoring, simulation, and optimization. Digital twin technology enables manufacturers to create virtual models of robotic systems, analyze performance data, and predict potential failures before they occur. For instance, General Electric (GE) utilizes digital twins to enhance the efficiency of robotic assembly lines in aerospace and automotive manufacturing. By integrating real-time sensor data with AI-driven analytics, companies can achieve predictive maintenance, reducing equipment downtime and improving overall production efficiency.

Moreover, AI-driven robotics in Industry 4.0 has paved the way for predictive maintenance and self-learning robotic systems that can detect anomalies, diagnose issues, and optimize their own performance without human intervention. Predictive maintenance utilizes IoT sensors embedded in robotic systems to continuously monitor operational parameters such as temperature, vibration, and pressure. By analyzing these data points through AI algorithms, manufacturers can proactively address potential failures, minimizing unplanned downtimes and maximizing equipment lifespan. Siemens' MindSphere platform is an example of how AI-powered predictive maintenance is enhancing industrial robotics by providing real-time diagnostics and optimizing production workflows.

In addition to traditional manufacturing and logistics, robotics is also revolutionizing industries such as healthcare, construction, and agriculture in the Industry 4.0 era. In healthcare, robotic-assisted surgeries, automated pharmaceutical production, and AI-driven diagnostic robots are enhancing medical precision and patient outcomes. For instance, Da Vinci surgical robots allow for minimally invasive procedures with unparalleled precision, reducing recovery time and surgical risks. In construction, 3D-printing robots such as those developed by Apis Cor are enabling rapid and cost-effective housing solutions by printing entire buildings layer by layer. Meanwhile, in agriculture, autonomous drones and robotic harvesters are optimizing crop monitoring, planting, and irrigation, contributing to sustainable farming practices.

Despite its numerous advantages, the implementation of robotics in Industry 4.0 also presents challenges, including cyber security risks, high initial costs, workforce displacement, and the need for advanced skill sets. As industrial robots become more interconnected through IoT and cloud computing, they become vulnerable to cyber threats such as hacking, data breaches, and system manipulations. Ensuring robust cyber security protocols, such as block chain-based authentication and AI-driven threat detection, is crucial for protecting robotic infrastructure. Additionally, the transition to Industry 4.0 requires significant investment in robotic automation, making it essential for businesses to balance cost-effectiveness with long-term benefits. Workforce displacement due to automation is another critical concern, necessitating the up skilling and re skilling of employees to adapt to AI-driven industrial environments.

Looking ahead, the future of robotics in Industry 4.0 will be shaped by 5G-enabled robotics, swarm intelligence, and quantum computing. The deployment of 5G networks will enable ultra-fast, low-latency communication between industrial robots, facilitating seamless coordination in large-scale manufacturing operations. Swarm robotics, inspired by biological systems such as ant colonies, will enhance distributed decision-making, allowing groups of autonomous robots to work collaboratively in complex industrial settings. Additionally, quantum computing is expected to revolutionize AI-driven robotics by significantly accelerating data processing capabilities, optimizing industrial workflows, and solving complex logistical challenges.

Robotics in Industry 4.0 is driving unprecedented advancements in industrial automation, reshaping manufacturing, logistics, healthcare, and numerous other sectors. With AI, IoT, and cloud computing at its core, Industry 4.0 robotics is not only enhancing productivity and efficiency but also paving the way for autonomous, intelligent, and self-optimizing industrial systems. While challenges such as cyber security and workforce adaptation need to be addressed, the benefits of robotics in Industry 4.0 are poised to redefine the future of smart manufacturing and beyond.

Human-Robot Interaction (HRI)

Human-Robot Interaction (HRI) is an interdisciplinary field that focuses on developing and optimizing interactions between humans and robots to improve efficiency, safety, and usability across various applications, including industrial automation, healthcare, service robotics, and assistive technologies. As robots become more integrated into workplaces, homes, and public spaces, the ability to communicate, collaborate, and coexist with humans effectively has become a critical area of research. HRI combines principles from robotics, artificial intelligence (AI), psychology, human factors engineering, and cognitive science to design robots that can perceive, interpret, and respond to human intentions, emotions, and actions in real time. With the rise of Industry 4.0 and autonomous systems, modern HRI technologies leverage natural language processing (NLP), computer vision, machine learning, haptic feedback, and social robotics to create seamless human-machine interactions.

One of the key aspects of HRI is collaborative robotics (cobots), which enables robots to work alongside human operators in shared workspaces without the need for physical barriers. Unlike traditional industrial robots, which are confined to cages for safety reasons, cobots are designed with advanced sensing capabilities, force-limiting actuators, and AI-driven predictive control systems to prevent collisions and adapt to dynamic environments. Companies such as Universal Robots, KUKA, and ABB have developed cobots that assist in tasks such as assembly, packaging, and quality inspection, significantly improving productivity and ergonomics in manufacturing. These robots rely on real-time gesture recognition, speech commands, and proximity sensors to understand human intentions and adjust their behavior accordingly. By reducing the cognitive and physical workload of human workers, cobots enhance workplace safety, minimize errors, and increase overall efficiency.

Another critical area of HRI is social robotics, which focuses on developing robots that can engage with humans in social and assistive roles. Social robots are commonly used in healthcare, customer service, education, and eldercare to provide companionship, therapy, and assistance. These robots are designed with human-like facial expressions, speech synthesis, and emotion recognition capabilities to establish more natural and meaningful interactions. For example, SoftBank's Pepper robot is equipped with AI-powered speech recognition and facial detection to interact with customers in retail environments, while PARO, a robotic seal, is used in therapy sessions for patients with dementia and autism. Social robots are also gaining traction in educational settings, where they assist teachers in personalized learning and language acquisition for children. Research in this domain explores how humans perceive robotic social cues, trust robotic decisions, and respond to long-term interactions with AI-driven robots.

A significant challenge in HRI is ensuring intuitive and user-friendly communication between humans and robots. Traditional robot programming requires technical expertise, but advances in natural language processing (NLP) and multimodal interaction have enabled users to communicate with robots using voice commands, touch screens, gestures, and even brain-computer interfaces (BCIs). Google's Dialogflow, OpenAI's ChatGPT, and Amazon's Alexa AI have made significant progress in voice-based interactions, allowing robots to understand contextual language, execute complex tasks, and provide meaningful feedback. Gesture and gaze tracking systems further enhance interaction by enabling robots to detect non-verbal cues and adjust their responses based on human behavior. These advancements make HRI more accessible and reduce the learning curve for non-expert users, facilitating widespread adoption in various industries.

Another major research area in HRI is human trust and ethical considerations in robotic interactions. As robots take on increasingly autonomous roles, it is crucial to understand how humans develop trust in robotic systems and how biases in AI can impact decision-making. Studies have shown that users tend to trust robots that exhibit predictable behavior, transparency in decision-making, and the ability to explain their actions. The concept of explainable AI (XAI) is becoming essential in HRI, ensuring that robots can provide justifications for their decisions, especially in critical applications such as autonomous driving, medical diagnosis, and military robotics. Additionally, ethical concerns surrounding privacy, data security, and job displacement must be addressed to foster a positive relationship between humans and robots. Regulatory bodies and organizations such as IEEE, ISO, and the European Commission are developing ethical guidelines for responsible AI and robotic deployments, emphasizing transparency, accountability, and inclusivity in HRI design.

In the future, HRI will be shaped by emerging technologies such as 5G communication, edge computing, and bio-inspired robotics. The integration of brain-computer interfaces (BCIs) could enable seamless control of robotic systems through neural signals, opening new possibilities for assistive technologies and neuro prosthetics. Advances in haptic feedback and soft robotics will further enhance physical human-robot interactions, allowing robots to exhibit lifelike touch sensitivity and adaptive movement. Furthermore, swarm robotics and multi-agent systems will enable robots to work collectively, learning from human guidance while optimizing complex tasks in real time. The ultimate goal of HRI is to develop robotic systems that are not only functionally efficient but also socially acceptable, emotionally intelligent, and ethically responsible. As robotics continues to evolve, achieving harmonious human-robot collaboration will be key to unlocking the full potential of intelligent automation. Whether in industrial settings, healthcare, education, or everyday life, the success of HRI will depend on designing robots that understand, adapt to, and enhance human experiences in a meaningful way.

Safety, Ethics, and Legal Implications

As robotics and artificial intelligence (AI) become increasingly integrated into industrial, medical, military, and consumer applications, concerns regarding safety, ethics, and legal implications have gained significant attention. Ensuring that robots operate safely and ethically while complying with regulatory frameworks is critical to fostering trust, minimizing risks and preventing potential harm to humans and society. The complexity of robotic decision-making, human-robot interaction (HRI), and autonomous systems requires comprehensive guidelines that address issues such as accident prevention, accountability, privacy, bias, and long-term societal impact. Researchers, policymakers, and industry leaders are actively working to establish standards and regulations that govern robotic autonomy while maintaining human oversight.

Safety Considerations in Robotics

One of the foremost concerns in robotics is safety, especially in environments where humans and robots coexist. Industrial robots, such as robotic arms used in manufacturing, have historically been confined to caged environments to prevent unintended human contact. However, the advent of collaborative robots (cobots) and autonomous mobile robots (AMRs) necessitates the development of advanced safety mechanisms to minimize risks. These include proximity sensors, computer vision, force-limiting actuators, and AI-driven predictive control systems that allow robots to detect and respond to potential hazards in real time. Safety standards such as ISO 10218 (Robots and Robotic Devices—Safety Requirements for Industrial Robots) and ISO/TS 15066 (Safety Guidelines for Collaborative Robots) define best practices for ensuring safe human-robot collaboration.

In autonomous driving and robotic transportation systems, safety is paramount, as failure can result in serious injuries or fatalities. Self-driving cars, such as those developed by Tesla, Waymo, and General Motors, rely on AI-based perception systems to navigate roads and make split-second decisions. However, challenges such as sensor limitations, unpredictable human behavior, and adversarial attacks on AI models raise concerns about reliability. High-profile accidents involving autonomous vehicles have prompted regulatory agencies, such as the National Highway Traffic Safety Administration (NHTSA) and the European Commission, to demand rigorous safety evaluations before widespread deployment.

Ethical Considerations in Robotics

The ethical implications of robotics revolve around issues such as fairness, transparency, accountability, and societal impact. One major concern is algorithmic bias, where AI-powered robots may exhibit discriminatory behavior due to biased training data. For example, facial recognition systems in security robots have been criticized for racial and gender biases, leading to misidentifications and ethical dilemmas. Addressing this issue requires the implementation of fair AI training datasets, explainable AI (XAI), and ethical AI frameworks to ensure that robotic decision-making aligns with human values. Organizations such as the IEEE Global Initiative on Ethics of Autonomous and Intelligent Systems are actively developing guidelines for designing ethical AI in robotics.

Another ethical concern is autonomous decision-making in lethal applications, such as military drones and autonomous weapons. Countries and advocacy groups are debating the morality of allowing AI-driven robots to make life-and-death decisions without human intervention. The Campaign to Stop Killer Robots, backed by organizations like the United Nations (UN) and Human Rights Watch, advocates for an international ban on fully autonomous weapons to prevent potential misuse. Conversely, proponents argue that AI-powered defense systems could minimize collateral damage and improve battlefield precision compared to human decision-making. Balancing these perspectives requires clear ethical guidelines that emphasize human oversight, proportionality, and accountability in robotic warfare.

In healthcare, robotic systems such as surgical robots (e.g., Da Vinci system) and AI-driven diagnostic tools raise concerns about patient safety, medical liability, and the depersonalization of healthcare. While robotic-assisted surgeries enhance precision, who is legally responsible if a surgical robot malfunctions—the surgeon, the hospital, or the manufacturer? Ethical AI in healthcare must ensure patient consent, data privacy, and transparency in medical decision-making to maintain trust and ethical standards.

Legal and Regulatory Implications in Robotics

As robots take on more autonomous roles, legal frameworks must adapt to address liability, data protection, and compliance with safety standards. One of the most debated legal questions in robotics is liability in case of accidents or malfunctions. If an autonomous vehicle crashes, determining legal responsibility—whether it falls on the car manufacturer, software developer, AI system, or user—is challenging. Many countries are updating their legal systems to define AI accountability, with the European Union (EU) AI Act proposing clear regulations on AI transparency, risk assessment, and legal responsibilities.

Another key legal issue is data privacy and surveillance. Many robotic systems, including service robots, drones, and AI assistants, collect and process large amounts of personal data. Laws such as the General Data Protection Regulation (GDPR) in Europe and the California Consumer Privacy Act (CCPA) in the U.S. regulate how companies collect, store, and use biometric and behavioral data. Compliance with these laws is crucial to ensuring that robots do not violate privacy rights.

Furthermore, workforce displacement and labor laws are becoming pressing concerns as automation replaces traditional jobs. Governments and organizations must consider policies for worker retraining, AI-driven job augmentation, and economic restructuring to prevent large-scale unemployment. The World Economic Forum (WEF) has emphasized the need for "reskilling and upskilling" initiatives to prepare workers for the transition to a more automated future.

Future Directions in Robotics Safety, Ethics, and Law

To ensure safe, ethical, and legally compliant robotic systems, the future of robotics will likely include:

- Global AI and robotics governance: Establishing universal regulations on AI transparency, accountability, and safety.
- Explainable AI (XAI): Mandating that robotic systems provide clear, understandable justifications for their actions.
- Ethical AI Audits: Regular reviews of AI decision-making to prevent bias and discrimination.
- Cyber security advancements: Strengthening protections against AI hacking, data breaches, and adversarial attacks on robotic systems.
- Human-AI collaboration frameworks: Defining boundaries between human decision-making and robotic autonomy to maintain ethical responsibility and oversight.

Ensuring the safety, ethics, and legal compliance of robotics is essential for their responsible integration into society. As AI-powered robots take on more complex tasks, policymakers, engineers, and ethicists must work together to establish global standards that prioritize human well-being, security, and fairness. Only through a balanced approach that integrates innovation with ethical safeguards can robotics achieve its full potential while mitigating risks to individuals and society.

Challenges and Future Directions

As robotics continues to evolve and integrate into various industries, several key challenges must be addressed to enable widespread adoption and enhance the capabilities of robotic systems. One of the most pressing challenges is autonomous decision-making and adaptability. While modern robots leverage artificial intelligence (AI) and machine learning (ML) to improve their performance, they still struggle with uncertainty, unstructured environments, and real-time decision-making in dynamic scenarios. For instance, autonomous robots in search and rescue missions or self-driving vehicles must handle unpredictable obstacles, weather conditions, and human behavior, which remain difficult problems for current AI models. Explainable AI (XAI) is also a growing concern, as robots must provide transparent justifications for their decisions, particularly in critical areas such as healthcare, military applications, and finance.

Another significant challenge is robotic perception and sensor limitations. Although advancements in computer vision, LiDAR, and depth sensing have improved robots' ability to interpret their surroundings, these systems still struggle with object occlusion, poor lighting conditions, and adversarial attacks that can deceive AI models. Additionally, the integration of tactile sensing and haptic feedback remains a hurdle, as current robotic hands and grippers lack the fine dexterity and sensitivity needed for delicate tasks such as surgical operations, prosthetic control, and micro-assembly in electronics manufacturing. Future developments in bio-inspired robotics, neuromorphic computing, and soft robotics could enhance robots' ability to interact with their environment more naturally and effectively. A crucial concern in robotics is energy efficiency and power consumption, particularly for autonomous robots and drones that require prolonged operation. While lithium-ion batteries and wireless charging systems have improved, energy density and longevity remain bottlenecks, limiting robotic endurance in space exploration, underwater robotics, and long-term surveillance. Research into alternative energy sources, such as biofuel cells, energy-harvesting materials, and hydrogen fuel cells, is being explored to extend robotic operational time. For instance, NASA's Perseverance Rover on Mars utilizes a radioisotope thermoelectric generator (RTG) to sustain its mission for years, but such technology is not yet feasible for consumer and industrial robotics due to cost and safety concerns.

From a societal perspective, human-robot interaction (HRI) and ethical concerns pose significant challenges. As robots take on more roles in healthcare, customer service, and education, ensuring user trust, emotional intelligence, and cultural sensitivity is crucial. Social robots must be designed with inclusive AI models that respect diverse linguistic, gender, and ethical considerations. Furthermore, robotics in the workforce raises concerns about job displacement and economic disruption, necessitating policies for worker reskilling, AI-driven job augmentation, and ethical labor laws. Governments and organizations such as the World Economic Forum (WEF) are actively discussing the impact of automation on employment and the need for adaptive education models.

Future Directions in Robotics

Looking ahead, the future of robotics will be shaped by several emerging technologies and interdisciplinary innovations. One key area is the development of next-generation AI algorithms, incorporating neurosymbolic AI, reinforcement learning, and cognitive computing to enhance robots' reasoning, adaptability, and human-like decision-making. Additionally, 5G and edge computing will revolutionize real-time robotic communication, enabling swarm robotics and multi-agent collaboration in smart factories, autonomous transportation, and environmental monitoring.

Another transformative direction is brain-computer interfaces (BCIs) and human augmentation. Research in neuroprosthetics and direct neural control is paving the way for robotic systems that can be controlled through thought, benefiting individuals with disabilities and enabling advanced military applications. Companies like Neuralink, DARPA, and BrainGate are developing BCIs that could allow seamless human-robot collaboration, reducing reliance on traditional control interfaces. Furthermore, robotic miniaturization and nanotechnology are expected to revolutionize medicine and materials science. Nanorobots could be used for targeted drug delivery, cancer treatment, and deep-tissue diagnostics, allowing for non-invasive medical procedures that surpass the precision of current robotic-assisted surgeries. Similarly, advancements in programmable matter and shape-shifting robots could lead to self-repairing infrastructure, modular robotic systems, and reconfigurable materials.

Finally, space exploration and extraterrestrial robotics will continue to push the boundaries of robotics research. NASA, ESA, and private companies like SpaceX and Blue Origin are investing in autonomous rovers, robotic habitats, and AI-driven space probes to explore Mars, the Moon, and beyond. Robotic systems will play a crucial role in asteroid mining, lunar colonization, and deep-space exploration, requiring breakthroughs in radiation resistance, autonomous self-repair and interplanetary navigation. While robotics faces technical, ethical, and regulatory challenges, the field is advancing rapidly through AI, sensor technology, energy efficiency, and interdisciplinary innovation. By addressing these challenges and leveraging emerging technologies, robotics has the potential to reshape industries, enhance human capabilities, and revolutionize the way we interact with intelligent machines in the coming decades.

Conclusion and Future Outlook

Robotics has evolved from rigid, pre-programmed machines in controlled environments to intelligent, adaptive, and autonomous systems capable of interacting with humans and dynamic surroundings. The advancements in artificial intelligence (AI), machine learning (ML), computer vision, and human-robot interaction (HRI) have enabled robots to play critical roles in industries such as manufacturing, healthcare, agriculture, logistics, and defense and space exploration. As the world transitions into Industry 4.0, robotics will continue to drive automation, efficiency, and innovation, reshaping the global economy and workforce. However, this rapid progress also presents significant challenges, including safety concerns, ethical dilemmas, regulatory uncertainties, and potential social disruptions. Addressing these challenges requires a multidisciplinary approach involving engineers, policymakers, ethicists, and economists to ensure that robotics development aligns with human values and societal needs. Looking toward the future, the integration of AI with robotics will enable even greater autonomy and decision-making capabilities, paving the way for self-learning robots, bio-inspired robotic systems, and brain-computer interface (BCI) technologies that enhance human-robot collaboration. The development of soft robotics, nanorobots, and humanoid robots will expand applications in medicine, disaster response, and eldercare, revolutionizing healthcare and assistance for aging populations. Meanwhile, swarm robotics and multi-agent systems will enhance collaborative tasks, enabling robots to work in teams for applications such as environmental monitoring, precision agriculture, and autonomous transportation networks. Advances in quantum computing, 5G, and edge computing will also accelerate robotic performance, enabling faster decision-making and real-time responsiveness in complex environments.

However, ethical and regulatory considerations will play a crucial role in shaping the future of robotics. Governments and organizations worldwide must establish comprehensive policies on AI accountability, data privacy, and workforce transition strategies to mitigate the risks associated with widespread automation. Public acceptance and trust in robots will depend on their ability to operate transparently, safely, and ethically. Explainable AI (XAI), fair AI policies, and international cooperation will be vital in ensuring responsible deployment and governance of robotics technologies. In the long term, robotics will play a central role in space exploration, deep-sea research, smart cities, and sustainable infrastructure development. With increasing investments in autonomous drones, robotic exoskeletons, and humanoid assistants, the future of robotics is set to enhance human capabilities rather than replace them. By fostering ethical innovation, interdisciplinary collaboration, and responsible AI development, robotics will not only revolutionize industries but also improve the quality of life, enable scientific breakthroughs, and drive global progress in the decades to come.

Acknowledgement

We are very much thankful to the authors of different publications as many new ideas are abstracted from them. The authors are highly thankful to ...., Publishing Process Manager, ..., Academic Editor the Bhumi Publishing for providing the opportunity to publish this book chapter. Authors also express gratefulness to their colleagues and family members for their continuous help, inspirations, encouragement, and sacrifices without which the book chapter could not be executed. Finally, the main target of this book will not be achieved unless it is used by research institutions, students, research scholars, and authors in their future works. The authors will remain ever grateful to Dr. H. S. Ginwal, Director, ICFRE-Tropical Forest Research Institute, Jabalpur Principal, Jabalpur Engineering College, Jabalpur & Principal Government Science College, Jabalpur who helped by giving constructive suggestions for this work. The authors are also responsible for any possible errors and shortcomings, if any in the book, despite the best attempt to make it immaculate.

References

[1] Woolley, Samuel, and Philip Howard. Computational propaganda worldwide: Executive summary. (2017).

[2] Spong, M. W., Hutchinson, S., & Vidyasagar, M. (2020). Robot Modeling and Control (2nd ed.). Wiley.

[3] Craig, J. J. (2021). Introduction to Robotics: Mechanics and Control (4th ed.). Pearson.

[4] Sciavicco, L., & Siciliano, B. (2012). Modelling and Control of Robot Manipulators (2nd ed.). Springer.

[5] Paul, R. P. (1981). Robot Manipulators: Mathematics, Programming, and Control. MIT Press.

[6] Mishra, R.K. and Agarwal, R. (2024a), Artificial Intelligence in Material Science: Revolutionizing Construction, In: Research and Reviews in Material Science Volume I, ISBN: 978-93-95847-83-4, 69- 99.

[7] Mishra, R.K. and Agarwal, R. (2024b), Impact of digital evolution on various facets of computer science and information technology, In: Digital Evolution: Advances in Computer Science and Information Technology, First Edition: June 2024, ISBN: 978-93-95847-84-1.

[8] Mishra, R.K., Mishra, Divyansh and Agarwal, R. (2024c), An Artificial Intelligence-Powered Approach to Material Design, In: Cutting-Edge Research in Chemical and Material Science Volume I, First Edition: August 2024, ISBN: 978-93-95847-39-1.

[9] Mishra, R.K., Mishra, Divyansh and Agarwal, R. (2024d), Artificial Intelligence and Machine Learning in Research, In: Innovative Approaches in Science and Technology Research Volume I, First Edition: October 2024, ISBN: 978-81-979987-5-1

[10] Khalil, W., & Dombre, E. (2004). Modeling, Identification, and Control of Robots. Butterworth-Heinemann.

[11] Featherstone, R. (2008). Rigid Body Dynamics Algorithms. Springer.

[12] Murray, R. M., Li, Z., & Sastry, S. S. (1994). A Mathematical Introduction to Robotic Manipulation. CRC Press.

[13] Khatib, O. (1987). A Unified Approach for Motion and Force Control of Robot Manipulators. IEEE Journal on Robotics and Automation, 3(1), 43-53.

[14] Siciliano, B., & Khatib, O. (Eds.). (2016). Springer Handbook of Robotics (2nd ed.). Springer.

[15] Mishra, Divyansh, Mishra, R.K. and Agarwal, R. (2024e), Recent trends in artificial intelligence and its applications, In: Artificial Intelligence- Trends and Applications Volume I, First Edition: December 2024, ISBN: 978-93-95847-63-6.

[16] MIT OpenCourseWare – Introduction to Robotics (https://ocw.mit.edu/courses/mechanical-engineering/2-12-introduction-to-robotics-fall-2020/)

[17] Modern Robotics: Mechanics, Planning, and Control – Online Course by Northwestern University (https://modernrobotics.northwestern.edu/)

[18]   Xu, L. D., Xu, E. L., & Li, L. (2018). Industry 4.0: State of the art and future trends. International Journal of Production Research, 56(8), 2941-2962.

[19]   Kusiak, A. (2018). Smart manufacturing. International Journal of Production Research, 56(1-2), 508-517.

[20]   Schumacher, A., Erol, S., & Sihn, W. (2016). A maturity model for assessing Industry 4.0 readiness and maturity of manufacturing enterprises. Procedia CIRP, 52, 161-166.

[21]   Villani, V., Pini, F., Leali, F., & Secchi, C. (2018). Survey on human–robot collaboration in industrial settings: Safety, intuitive interfaces and applications. Mechatronics, 55, 248-266.

[22]   Universal Robots. (2021). Collaborative Robots in Smart Manufacturing. Retrieved from https://www.universal-robots.com

[23]   Wurman, P. R., D'Andrea, R., & Mountz, M. (2008). Coordinating hundreds of cooperative, autonomous vehicles in warehouses. AI Magazine, 29(1), 9-20.

[24]   Amazon Robotics. (2022). Autonomous Warehouse Solutions. Retrieved from https://www.amazonrobotics.com

[25]   Tao, F., Zhang, M., Liu, Y., & Nee, A. Y. C. (2019). Digital twin in industry: State-of-the-art. IEEE Transactions on Industrial Informatics, 15(4), 2405-2415.

[26]   Siemens. (2021). Digital Twins in Smart Factories. Retrieved from https://www.siemens.com

[27]   Lee, J., Kao, H. A., & Yang, S. (2014). Service innovation and smart analytics for Industry 4.0 and big data environment. Procedia CIRP, 16, 3-8.

[28]   Siemens MindSphere. (2022). AI-Powered Predictive Maintenance for Industrial Automation.   Retrieved   from https://www.siemens.com/mindsphere

[29]   Apis Cor. (2021). 3D-Printed Construction with Robotic Automation. Retrieved from https://www.apis-cor.com

[30]   Intuitive Surgical. (2022). Da Vinci Surgical System in Modern Healthcare. Retrieved   from   https://www.intuitive.com/en-us/products-and-services/da-vinci

[31]   Chamoso, P., González-Briones, A., Rodríguez, S., & Corchado, J. M. (2020). Tendencies of technologies and platforms in smart agriculture: A state-of-the-art review. Computers and Electronics in Agriculture, 170, 105225.

[32]   Humayed, A., Lin, J., Li, F., & Luo, B. (2017). Cyber-physical systems security— A survey. IEEE Internet of Things Journal, 4(6), 1802-1831.

[33]   Blockchain for Cyber security in Industry 4.0. (2021). IBM Research. Retrieved from https://www.ibm.com/blockchain

[34]   Fawzi, A., Fawzi, H., & Camenisch, J. (2018). Quantum-secure authentication and key-exchange. IEEE Transactions on Information Theory, 64(7), 4802-4820.

[35]   Swarm Robotics in Industry 4.0. (2021). Boston Dynamics Research Lab. Retrieved from https://www.bostondynamics.com

[36]   5G and Robotics: Ericsson Industry Reports. (2022). Retrieved from https://www.ericsson.com/en/5g